SCHOLASTIC

READ & RESPOND

Helping children discover the pleasure and power of reading

LOOK UP!

by Nathan Bryon   illustrated by Dapo Adeola

FOR AGES 5–7

Published in the UK by Scholastic, 2023

Scholastic Distribution Centre, Bosworth Avenue, Tournament Fields, Warwick, CV34 6UQ

Scholastic Ireland, 89E Lagan Road, Dublin Industrial Estate, Glasnevin, Dublin, D11 HP5F

SCHOLASTIC and associated logos are trademarks and/or registered trademarks of Scholastic Inc.

www.scholastic.co.uk

© 2023 Scholastic Limited

1 2 3 4 5 6 7 8 9   3 4 5 6 7 8 9 0 1 2

A CIP catalogue record for this book is available from the British Library.
ISBN 978-0702-32067-5

Printed and bound by Ashford Colour Press

The book is made of materials from well-managed, FSC®-certified forests and other controlled sources.

Extracts from *The National Curriculum in England, English Programme of Study* © Crown Copyright. Reproduced under the terms of the Open Government Licence (OGL). http://www.nationalarchives.gov.uk/doc/open-government-licence/version/3

Author Samantha Pope

Editorial team Rachel Morgan, Vicki Yates, Caroline Low, Liz Evans

Series designer Andrea Lewis

Typesetter QBS Learning

Illustrator Lays Bittencourt

Photographs page 14: Mae Jemison, IanDagnall Computing/Alamy Stock Photo; page 20: space cheeseburger, NASA Image Collection/Alamy Stock Photo; page 29: meteor shower, Belish/Shutterstock

Acknowledgements

The publishers gratefully acknowledge permission to reproduce the following copyright material: **Penguin Random House UK** for the use of the Extract and illustrations from *Look Up!* by Nathan Bryon, text copyright © 2019 Nathan Bryon, illustrations copyright © 2019 Dapo Adeola.

Every effort has been made to trace copyright holders for the works reproduced in this book, and the publishers apologise for any inadvertent omissions.

For supporting online resources go to:
www.scholastic.co.uk/read-and-respond/books/look-up/online-resources
Access key: Finally

CONTENTS ▼

How to use Read & Respond in your classroom...

Read & Respond provides teaching ideas related to a specific well-loved children's book. Each Read & Respond book is divided into the following sections:

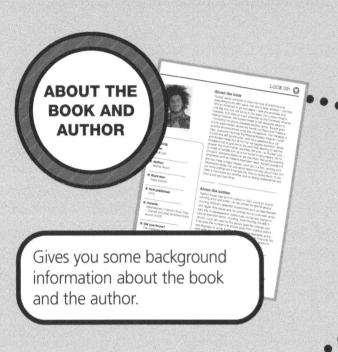

ABOUT THE BOOK AND AUTHOR

Gives you some background information about the book and the author.

GUIDED READING

Breaks the book down into sections and gives notes for using it, ideal for use with the whole class. A bookmark has been provided on page 10 containing **comprehension** questions. The children can be directed to refer to these as they read. Find comprehensive guided reading sessions in the supporting online resources.

SHARED READING

Provides extracts from the children's book with associated notes for focused work. There is also one non-fiction extract that relates to the children's book.

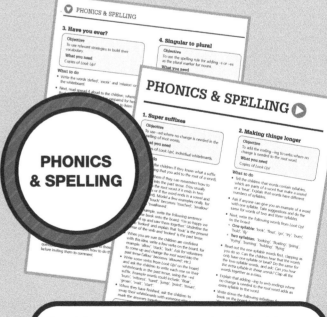

PHONICS & SPELLING

Provides word-level work related to the children's book so you can teach phonics, spelling and **vocabulary** in context.

PLOT, CHARACTER & SETTING

Contains activity ideas focused on the plot, characters and the setting of the story.

🛈 PLOT, CHARACTER & SETTING

Space menu

In space, astronauts eat three main meals a day like we do on Earth. But, as there is no gravity, they have to eat their food differently.

Some foods can be eaten fresh, like fruit, but main meals come ready-made in packets that astronauts add water to.

Astronauts can choose from lots of different foods, including their favourites. British astronaut Tim Peake asked a famous chef to make him a special bacon sandwich that he could take to space!

However, bread isn't good in space because crumbs can get into the equipment. Instead, flatbreads are used. That is how astronaut Terry Virts created his very own 'space cheeseburger' – by putting beef, cheese, tomato paste and mustard into a wrap!

Most drinks are allowed on board. If an astronaut wants milk or sugar in their tea or coffee, it has to be added before blast-off: you cannot stir milk and sugar into a cup of tea in space!

A space cheeseburger

• What would you want to eat in space? On a piece of paper, write down your choices for breakfast, lunch and dinner – together with your favourite snacks and drinks.

20 Read & Respond Look Up!

TALK ABOUT IT

Oracy, **fluency**, and speaking and listening activities. These activities may be based directly on the children's book or be broadly based on the themes and concepts of the story.

Provides writing activities related to the children's book. These activities may be based directly on the children's book or be broadly based on the themes and concepts of the story.

GET WRITING

ASSESSMENT

Contains short activities that will help you assess whether the children have understood concepts and curriculum objectives. They are designed to be informal activities to feed into your planning.

Online you can find a host of supporting documents including planning information, comprehensive guided reading sessions and guidance on teaching reading.

www.scholastic.co.uk/read-and-respond/books/look-up/online-resources

Access key: Finally

SUPPORTING ONLINE RESOURCE

Help children develop a love of reading for pleasure.

Activities

The activities follow the same format:

- **Objective:** the objective for the lesson. It will be based upon a curriculum objective, but will often be more specific to the focus being covered.

- **What you need:** a list of resources you need to teach the lesson, including photocopiable pages.

- **What to do:** the activity notes.

- **Differentiation:** this is provided where specific and useful differentiation advice can be given to support and/or extend the learning in the activity. Differentiation by providing additional adult support has not been included as this will be at a teacher's discretion based upon specific children's needs and ability, as well as the availability of support.

The activities are numbered for reference within each section and should move through the text sequentially – so you can use the lesson while you are reading the book. Once you have read the book, most of the activities can be used in any order you wish.

CURRICULUM LINKS

Section	Activity	Curriculum objectives
Guided reading		Comprehension: To participate in discussion about what is read to them, taking turns and listening to what others say; to explain clearly their understanding of what is read to them.
Shared reading	1	Comprehension: To draw on what the children already know or on background information and vocabulary provided by the teacher.
	2	Comprehension: To discuss and clarify the meaning of words, linking new meanings to known vocabulary.
	3	Comprehension: To listen to and discuss a wide range of poems, stories and non-fiction.
Phonics & spelling	1	Transcription (Spelling): To use –ed where no change is needed in the spelling of root words.
	2	Transcription (Spelling): To add the ending –ing to verbs where no change is needed to the root word.
	3	Spoken language: To use relevant strategies to build their vocabulary.
	4	Transcription (Spelling): To use the spelling rule for adding –s or –es as the plural marker for nouns.
Plot, character & setting	1	Spoken language: To listen and respond appropriately to adults and their peers.
	2	Comprehension: To discuss the significance of events.
	3	Composition: To read aloud their writing clearly enough to be heard by their peers and the teacher.
	4	Comprehension: To make inferences on the basis of what is being said and done.
	5	Comprehension: To participate in discussion about what is read to them, taking turns and listening to what others say.
	6	Spoken language: To articulate and justify answers, arguments and opinions.
Talk about it	1	Comprehension: To link what they read or hear to their own experiences.
	2	Spoken language: To gain, maintain and monitor the interest of the listener(s).
	3	Spoken language: To participate in discussions, presentations, performances, role play, improvisations and debates.
	4	Spoken language: To consider and evaluate different viewpoints, attending to and building on the contributions of others.
	5	Spoken language: To give well-structured descriptions, explanations and narratives for different purposes, including for expressing feelings.
	6	Spoken language: To ask relevant questions to extend their understanding and knowledge.
Get writing	1	Comprehension: To explain clearly their understanding of what is read to them.
	2	Vocabulary, grammar and punctuation: To begin to punctuate sentences using a capital letter and a full stop, question mark or exclamation mark.
	3	Composition: To discuss what they have written with the teacher or other pupils.
	4	Composition: To write sentences by composing a sentence orally before writing it.
	5	Composition: To sequence sentences to form short narratives.
	6	Composition: To consider what they are going to write before beginning by encapsulating what they want to say, sentence by sentence.
Assessment	1	Vocabulary, grammar and punctuation: To learn how to use expanded noun phrases to describe and specify.
	2	Word reading: To read words with contractions [for example, I'm, I'll, we'll], and understand that the apostrophe represents the omitted letter(s).
	3	Vocabulary, grammar and punctuation: To develop their understanding of the concepts set out in English Appendix 2 by joining words and joining clauses using 'and'.
	4	Comprehension: To discuss and clarify the meaning of words, linking new meanings to known vocabulary.

Key facts

⦿ **Title:**
Look Up!

_____

⦿ **Author:**
Nathan Bryon

_____

⦿ **Illustrator:**
Dapo Adeola

_____

⦿ **First published:**
2019

_____

⦿ **Awards:**
Waterstones Children's Book Prize – Overall, and best illustrated book award (2020)

_____

⦿ **Did you know?**
The character of Rocket is based on one of Dapo Adeola's nieces

About the book

Rocket wants everyone to share her love of anything and everything to do with space. Her idol is Mae Jemison – the first African American to go into space – and she promises that one day she, too, will be up in the stars! Her current mission, however, is to draw attention to the imminent Phoenix Meteor Shower. She is determined to tell everyone about it – including her phone-obsessed brother Jamal. Rocket goes to the supermarket, where she hands out flyers and makes a surprise announcement using the microphone. Her message is clear: Everyone must see the Phoenix Meteor Shower! Jamal is cross but still ignoring her, until he is splashed by a car and Rocket makes fun of him for not paying attention. Jamal threatens not to take her to the park that evening to see the shower, but their mother overrides him and – to Rocket's joy – a crowd of people turn up at her house to accompany her to the park. Everyone dashes to see the show, but as the evening progresses and no meteors have been seen, Rocket wonders if she has made a huge mistake. *Look Up!* is a fun, exciting and informative book, not only about space but also about how rich our surroundings are if we take the time to notice them. It also takes a humorous but sensitive look at sibling relationships and their good and bad times.

_____

About the author

Nathan Bryon was born in London in 1991 and is an award-winning actor and writer. He has written for BAFTA-award-winning children's television programmes such as *Swashbuckle* and *Apple Tree House* and he currently has an animated series, *Afro Kid*, in development. Additionally, he has also starred in various television series, including the BBC's *Ghosts*.

   Look Up! was his first picture book for children and it became the number-one picture book from a debut author and illustrator in 2019. It was a *Sunday Times* bestseller and it won both the overall Waterstones Children's Book Prize and the illustrated book award in 2020. There are two more books in the series featuring Rocket.

_____

About the illustrator

Dapo Adeola was born in Britain, of Nigerian heritage. At school, he decided that he wanted to go into a career in graphic design and studied art at GCSE and A Level before starting a foundation art degree that included fine art, graphic design and photography. However, illustration was not included, so he learned through online courses and started sharing his work on Instagram, where he met Nathan Bryon. Dapo says that he wishes to challenge gender and racial norms through his work in a fun way.

GUIDED READING ▶

Getting the most from the book

The book makes much use of typography – with many exclamation marks, questions and emboldened words. Where you see this, ensure that your expression, when reading aloud, matches the desired aim for the story. Draw the children's attention to these examples and explain how the use of these features adds to the book's excitement.

Front and back covers

Together, as a class, look at the front and back covers of the book before you start reading the story. Draw the children's attention to both the words and the illustrations. Ask question 1 on the bookmark: *Why is the book called* Look Up!*?*

Spreads 1–3

Explain to the children, as you read through the first few spreads, that their purpose is to establish the scene, setting, characters and what the book is about. On the first page, we see Rocket in her bedroom. Ask the children question 3 on the bookmark: *How can you tell that Rocket is interested in space from the illustrations?* (Apart from the telescope, there are stars on her wallpaper, pyjamas and curtains, she has star earrings, there is a spaceman on her bookshelf and there are drawings of the sun and the moon, etc.)

Look at spread 2, where we see Rocket's family. Ask the children how old they think Jamal is and why. (A teenager – he has some stubble on his chin and an earring and is fixated on his phone.) Next, highlight the words 'floating in the clouds' on the left page. Why are they not on the same line as the rest of the sentence? (They show that Rocket is a dreamer with her head in the clouds. They also look like they are floating, reflecting what the text says.) On the right-hand page, LOOK UP and LOOKS DOWN are written in bold capitals: why? (to establish early on the main difference between Rocket and Jamal)

In spread 3, we learn that Rocket's mother named her after a famous rocket that blasted into space on the day she was born. Ask the children: *What do you think this tells us about Rocket's mother?* (She probably shares her daughter's love of space and maybe this is how Rocket's interest started.)

On the right-hand page, we are introduced to Mae Jemison. Ask the children why she would want to go into space if she is scared of heights (perhaps to conquer the fear). Ask the children if they are scared of anything and what they could do to overcome it.

Spreads 4–5

In spread 4, Rocket says she has done everything to prepare for going into space. How does she defy gravity? (By going on a swing, she's in the air, not on the ground – but not *really* defying gravity!) She also says she has captured 'rare and exotic life forms' – is what she has caught rare? (not for Earth – a butterfly) On the right-hand page, she is holding a press meeting. Can the children guess, from the picture, what a press meeting is? (where someone makes an important announcement – you might have to explain what the 'press' are) Rocket has also made flyers – do the children know what they are?

In spread 5, Rocket and Jamal are walking to the supermarket. Ask the children: *Do you think the supermarket sells astronaut food?* (Unlikely!) Draw the children's attention to the other people in the street. Ask the children question 6 on the bookmark: *What are the other people doing as they walk down the street?* (They are busy looking down or at their phones or newspaper.) Ask the children if this is what it's like when they walk in the street – or do people look up more?

Spreads 6–8

In spread 6, they have arrived at the supermarket and Rocket is handing out her flyers to people. Ask the children: *Do you think the people look interested?* (They look more interested than Jamal!)

Focus on the left-hand page, with the 'Did you know' speech bubbles. Ask the children question 4 on the bookmark: *Why are facts in the book always in the speech bubbles?* (This helps them stand out more/makes them more noticeable.) Do the children find the facts interesting? Have any of them ever seen a meteor shower? On the right-hand page, Rocket grabs the microphone when no one is looking. Ask: *Is this a good thing to do or is it naughty?*

In spread 7, Rocket makes her announcement using the microphone. The spread itself is divided into three sections – Rocket on the far left, the supermarket customers in the middle, and Jamal on the right. Ask the children: Why has the illustrator done this? (perhaps to show again how different Rocket and Jamal are – they are opposites, in a way) Ask the children how they think Cathy, the shop assistant, feels when she takes the microphone off Rocket. Would she be annoyed that Rocket didn't ask permission first? Ask the children question 8 on the bookmark: *Why does Rocket think 'Jamal might be a tiny bit cross with me'?* (She took the microphone without asking/she embarrassed him, etc.)

In spread 8, after Jamal gets sprayed by a car driving through a puddle, Rocket laughs and says it was his fault for not looking up. Ask the children if they think she is being unkind. How do they think Jamal is feeling, judging by his body language in the illustrations?

Spreads 9–12

Rocket's mum insists that Jamal take his sister to the park in spread 9. Ask the children question 2 on the bookmark: *What does Rocket mean when she says her mum saves the day?* (that she helps calm or resolve the situation so Rocket can go to the park) How does Jamal feel about this, especially when Rocket does her 'famous victory dance'? Ask the children if they think Rocket is being irritating!

In spreads 10 and 11, everyone heads off to the park. Ask the children question 9 on the bookmark: *From the illustrations, how can we tell that everyone is excited about the meteor shower?* (People have big smiles on their faces, their arms are open, often raised, and they are looking at the sky.)

Compare the way the people look in those spreads to spread 12. What has changed? (Their expressions look less hopeful – some look puzzled or bored. Their arms drop and some have their

hands on their hips.) Draw the children's attention to the way the author uses repetition here. Ask the children question 7 on the bookmark: *What effect does repeating the words 'wait' and 'maybe' three times have on the story?* (We realise how long everyone is waiting and their growing suspicion nothing will happen. It also increases Rocket's sadness at the missing shower.) Ask the children to look at Jamal's expression on the right-hand page. How is he feeling now? (He feels sorry/concerned for her.)

Spreads 13–16

In spread 13, Jamal and Rocket are both in the same 'shot' of the spread, rather than being at opposite sides. What might this tell us about them? (that their relationship might be getting closer) Ask the children question 10 on the bookmark: *What is the importance of Jamal turning off his phone?* (This is huge – the biggest sign of concern or respect that he could have for his sister.) Rocket also apologises – ask the children why. (She realises that she has made this day all about her dreams without thinking of how others might feel.)

Spread 14 consists of just two words: 'LOOK UP!!!' Ask the children what effect this has on the book. (We can see from the faces there is something amazing to see – we know they are going to see the meteor shower.)

In spreads 15 and 16, we see Jamal and Rocket enjoying the meteor shower together. Ask the children question 5 on the bookmark: *How is the relationship between Rocket and Jamal different at the end of the book to the beginning?* (They are sitting/lying together on the grass, smiling, drinking hot chocolate. They like each other and appear much closer.) Look at the first sentence on the final page: 'I'm so happy we looked up and saw them together.' What does Rocket mean by this? (She realises that it's more fun to share her interests than to just think about them on her own.)

Look Up!
by Nathan Bryon & Dapo Adeola

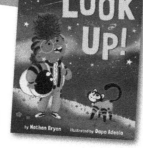

Focus on... Meaning

1. Why is the book called *Look Up!*?

2. What does Rocket mean when she says her mum saves the day?

Focus on... Organisation

3. How can you tell that Rocket is interested in space from the illustrations?

4. Why are facts in the book always in the speech bubbles?

5. How is the relationship between Rocket and Jamal different at the end of the book to the beginning?

Helping children discover the pleasure and power of reading

Look Up!
by Nathan Bryon & Dapo Adeola

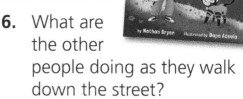

Focus on... Language and features

6. What are the other people doing as they walk down the street?

7. What effect does repeating the words 'wait' and 'maybe' three times have on the story?

Focus on... Purpose, viewpoints and effects

8. Why does Rocket think 'Jamal might be a tiny bit cross with me'?

9. From the illustrations, how can we tell that everyone is excited about the meteor shower?

10. What is the importance of Jamal turning off his phone?

Helping children discover the pleasure and power of reading

SHARED READING ▶

Extract 1

- Display an enlarged copy of Extract 1 and read it aloud. Ask the children: *How is Rocket feeling?* (She's excited – especially when people turn up at the house)

- Next, circle the words 'grab', 'grumbles', 'yell at the top of my lungs' and model how you would use them in sentences. Do the children know what they mean?

- Tell the children you are going to play a game called 'Three Times'. In this game, each child must think of three times when: they have grabbed something; they have grumbled; they have yelled at the top of their lungs.

- Model the answers yourself first, then ask the children to share their answers at the end. Ask them to expand on their answers and see if they can relate their feelings to those of Rocket and Jamal.

Extract 2

- Display an enlarged copy of Extract 2 and read through it with the class.

- Circle the words 'I've never, ever felt this sad before.' Ask: *Why is Rocket sadder about this than anything else?* (She is disappointed because the meteor shower hasn't happened and she was looking forward to it.) Ask if she might be feeling any other emotions. (She might also feel embarrassed because she made such a fuss about the shower and involved so many people.) Do the children think her reaction is understandable?

- Next, circle what Jamal says, 'I've turned my phone off, sis,' and ask why this is important. (We know that Jamal is always 'glued' to his phone and pays it more attention than he does anything else, so this shows that he understands how Rocket is feeling and wants to help.)

- On the next page, circle the word 'Suddenly', which is in a much larger font and in bold. Ask the children: *Why did the author want this word to stand out so much?* (to increase tension and expectation – and it also helps to lighten the sadness of the previous page)

Extract 3

- Tell the children that they are going to learn about the astronaut Mae Jemison.

- On the interactive whiteboard, show pictures of Mae Jemison from a young age up to nowadays.

- Ask the children what they can remember about Mae Jemison from *Look Up!* and why she's inspirational to Rocket.

- Next, read through Extract 3 with the children, explaining any new words. You might also need to explain *Star Trek* unless they know of the series or films.

- Ask the children if they think becoming an astronaut sounds easy. Would they like to be an astronaut? Why or why not?

- What do they think of Mae Jemison never going back to space again? Do they think she should have?

- Finally, read the quotation at the end and explain any words the children do not understand (for example, 'limitations'). Do they agree with what Mae thinks?

Extract 1

I grab my jet-pack rucksack, but Jamal is still glued to his game.

"Wait till I've completed the level, Rocket!" he grumbles.

As we're about to leave, the doorbell rings...

WOWSERS!

Everyone's here, and they're all holding my flyers.

"TO THE PARK!"

I yell at the top of my lungs. We're all so excited!

Extract 2

I've never, ever felt this sad before.

Jamal looks at me for the first time today. It feels like the first time ever.

"I've turned my phone off, sis," he says.

"I'm sorry for making you wait in the freezing cold for nothing, Jamal. Let's go home."

Suddenly there's a big bright light in the sky!

Extract 3

Star-struck

Mae Jemison was born in the USA on 17 October 1956. Ever since she was a very young girl, she spent a lot of time in her school library, reading books about science and astronomy.

When she was 12 years old, she watched Neil Armstrong become the first man to walk on the moon. It was exciting, but she was also sad because there were no women astronauts. She found a female role model in the television series *Star Trek*, with the character Nyota Uhura, who was played by actress Nichelle Nichols.

In 1987, after graduating with degrees in engineering and medicine, Mae Jemison was one of 2000 people who applied for NASA's astronaut training programme. Only 15 were accepted – and Mae Jemison was one of them!

On 12 September 1992, Jemison finally went into space with six other astronauts in the spaceship *Endeavour*. In eight days, the spaceship made 127 orbits around the Earth before returning home. Every time she made radio contact with people, she would greet them with Uhura's famous saying: "Hailing frequencies open."

Jemison left NASA in 1993 to teach at a university. She also started her own company to encourage young people to love science. One of the most famous things she said was: "Never be limited by other people's limited imaginations."

PHONICS & SPELLING ▶

1. Super suffixes

> **Objective**
> To use –ed where no change is needed in the spelling of root words.
>
> **What you need**
> Copies of *Look Up!*, individual whiteboards.

What to do

- First, ask the children if they know what a suffix is (an ending that you add to the root of a word).

- Next, ask them if they can remember how to put a verb into the past tense. (You usually add –ed to the root word if it ends in two consonants or if the word ends in a vowel and a consonant). Model a few examples orally, for example: 'touch' becomes 'touched', 'swallow' becomes 'swallowed'.

- As an example, write the following sentence from the book onto the board: 'I'm so happy we looked up and saw them together.' Underline the verb 'looked' and explain that 'look' is the present tense of the verb and 'looked' is the past tense.

- When you are sure the children are confident with this idea, write a few verbs on the board, for example: 'allow', 'crack', 'lock'. Ask for volunteers to come up and change the root word into the past tense ('allow' becomes 'allowed', etc.).

- Write some verbs from *Look Up!* on the board and ask the children to write each one on their whiteboards in the past tense, using the –ed suffix. Example words could include: 'float', 'burn', 'witness', 'hand', 'jump', 'point', 'moan', 'groan', 'wait', 'start'.

- When they have finished, ask the children to swap their whiteboards with someone else and mark the answers together.

> **Differentiation**
> **Extension:** Children could write short sentences including the words they have written.

2. Making things longer

> **Objective**
> To add the ending –ing to verbs where no change is needed to the root word.
>
> **What you need**
> Copies of *Look Up!*

What to do

- Tell the children that words contain syllables, which are parts of a word that make a sound or a 'beat'. Explain that words have different numbers of syllables.

- Ask if anyone can give you an example of a word with one syllable. Take suggestions and do the same for words of two and three syllables.

- Next, write the following words from *Look Up!* on the board:
  - **One syllable:** 'look', 'float', 'go', 'try', 'burn', 'hold', 'fly'
  - **Two syllables:** 'looking', 'floating', 'going', 'trying', 'burning', 'holding', 'flying'

- Read out the one-syllable words first, clapping as you do so. Can the children hear that the words only have one syllable or beat? Do the same for the two-syllable words, and ask: *Can you hear the extra syllable in these words?* Clap all the words together as a class.

- Explain that adding –ing to verb endings where no change is needed to the root word adds an extra syllable to the word.

- Write down the following infinitives from the book on the board: 'see', 'think', 'jump', 'wait', 'ring', 'yell', 'point', 'moan', 'groan'.

- Ask for volunteers to put these words into two syllables, saying the word and clapping the syllables at the same time: 'seeing', 'thinking', 'jumping', 'waiting', 'ringing', 'yelling', 'pointing', 'moaning', 'groaning'.

3. Have you ever?

Objective
To use relevant strategies to build their vocabulary.

What you need
Copies of *Look Up!*

What to do

- Write the words 'defied', 'exotic' and 'mission' on the whiteboard.

- Next, read spread 4 aloud to the children, where Rocket talks about how she has prepared for her career as an astronaut. Tell the children to listen out for the three words on the board.

- Return to the vocabulary and provide the children with a definition for each word, putting them into a sentence that is different to the one used in the story. For example:
  - *The verb 'defied' (or 'defy') means when you refuse to do something you're supposed to do.*
  - *'Exotic' is an adjective that describes things that are unusual or exciting because they are different to what we know in our everyday lives.*
  - *The word 'mission' means an important job or activity. For example, Rocket's mission is to tell everybody about the Phoenix Meteor Shower.*

- Once you feel confident that the children understand the meanings of the words, tell them you are going to play a game called 'Have You Ever…?' Write the following questions on the board:
  - *Have you ever defied someone? Tell us about a time when you didn't do as you were told, and use the word 'defied' in your answer.*
  - *What kind of things have you seen, tasted, touched or heard that we might think are exotic? Use the word 'exotic' in your answer.*
  - *Have you ever been on a mission? What important thing did you have to do? Tell me all about it, using the word 'mission' in your answer.*

- You could model your own answers to these questions to show the children how to do this before inviting them to comment.

4. Singular to plural

Objective
To use the spelling rule for adding –s or –es as the plural marker for nouns.

What you need
Copies of *Look Up!*

What to do

- Ask the children if they know the rule for making noun endings plural. (If the ending sounds like 's' or 'z', then add an 's' at the end of the word. If it sounds like 'iz', then add 'es'.) You might like to give a few examples of each to ensure the children understand the rule.

- Next, write up on the board all or some of the following nouns from the book: 'head', 'phone', 'rocket', 'astronaut', 'supermarket', 'shower', 'comet', 'grain', 'microphone', 'rucksack', 'game', 'doorbell', 'neck', 'plane', 'light', 'cup', 'hill'.

- Read each one aloud and ask the children how you should make them plural. (You just add an 's' to the end of each one.)

- Now, try it the other way around! Tell the children you want to make the following plural words from the book singular: 'flyers', 'lungs', 'telescopes', 'heights', 'clouds', 'meteors', 'birds'. How do you do it? (You just remove the final 's' from the word.)

- Finally, write up the following words on the board (explaining that these are not from the book!): 'box', 'flash', 'patch', 'peach'. Say each of them aloud and ask the children if they can tell you how to make them plural (you add 'es' to the end of the word). Can the children put the plural word into sentences? For example: 'The boxes of peaches were squashed.'

Differentiation

Extension: Challenge the children to look through the book and note down all plural nouns ending in 's'.

PLOT, CHARACTER & SETTING ▶

1. Moral of the story

> **Objective**
> To listen and respond appropriately to adults and their peers.
>
> **What you need**
> Copies of *Look Up!*
>
> **Cross-curricular link**
> PSHE

What to do

- Begin by telling children that many stories have a 'moral' or a 'message' in them. This is because an author wants the reader to come away from the book having learned or thought about an important point.

- Next, see if the children can give you any examples of stories where the main character or characters have learned an important lesson by the end. Ones you might suggest are traditional tales such as *Aesop's Fables* or *The Gingerbread Man*, where the moral of the story is: Don't trust strangers/Be careful who you trust. Write any examples and the morals on the board.

- You should also explain that bad things don't necessarily have to happen in stories with morals! The character might learn something positive such as how to overcome a problem or to believe in themselves.

- Next, ask the children: *What do you think the moral in* Look Up! *is?* Possible answers could include: taking time to look at the world around you instead of looking at your phone; being more aware of other people's feelings.

- Ask the children to create a *Look up!* 'moral' poster. Invite them to write their moral and illustrate it with an eye-catching picture.

2. All mixed up

> **Objective**
> To discuss the significance of events.
>
> **What you need**
> Copies of *Look Up!*, individual whiteboards.

What to do

- Before the lesson begins, write the following sentences onto the board, in a jumbled-up order:
  - *Jamal and Rocket drink hot chocolate and watch the meteors.*
  - *Rocket is excited to see the Phoenix Meteor Shower.*
  - *Jamal is cross and says he won't take Rocket to the park.*
  - *In the supermarket Rocket hands out flyers.*
  - *At first no one can see any meteors.*
  - *Mum says that Jamal must take Rocket to the park.*

- Explain to the children that stories are usually created to follow a specific order of events, so that the narrative makes sense as it progresses from start to finish. Tell the children that you are going to reread *Look Up!* together and that you want them to pay special attention to what happens in the book and when.

- Next, read out the sentences on the board and tell the children they are all jumbled up. Ask the children to work in groups to put them into the correct order and then call the class together to share their answers.

- In pairs, ask the children if they can retell the story of another book either that they have read as a class or in their own time. You could start them off by retelling a story that you know the children are familiar with and highlighting the main sequence of events.

3. Space menu

Objective

To read aloud their writing clearly enough to be heard by their peers and the teacher.

What you need

Copies of *Look Up!*, photocopiable page 20 'Space menu', websites with videos about astronaut food, blank paper and pens, astronaut food (optional!).

Cross-curricular links

Art and design, science

What to do

- Ask the children if they know what sort of food astronauts eat in space. Some children might talk about dried food that you have to add water to – which is correct! Much of an astronaut's diet will be in this form, though there is much more choice now than there used to be.

- If you can, search on the internet for 'what do astronauts eat in space for kids' and select 'videos'. There are plenty of fun and interesting short videos to show the children about what astronauts eat in space, which will be useful for this activity.

- Hand out photocopiable page 20 'Space menu'. Read it through with the children, explaining any difficult words. Ask what they think about space food. Does it sound yummy or disgusting?

- Next, hand out pieces of paper (lined or blank, according to your preference). Tell the children that you want them to plan a space menu for a day under the following headings: *Breakfast, Lunch, Dinner, Snacks, Drinks*.

- They should think about what they would like to eat and drink most if they were going into space; it seems most meals (with adaptations) are possible – even a cheeseburger! Children write their meals down under the headings and they can illustrate their menu, if they wish.

- If you have the budget, you could always order in a few packets of space food (easily found online) so children can see for themselves what it is like.

4. Forgive and forget?

Objective

To make inferences on the basis of what is being said and done.

What you need

Copies of *Look Up!*

Cross-curricular link

PSHE

What to do

- Look at spread 13 together, focusing on the left-hand page. Read aloud: "Jamal looks at me for the first time today. It feels like the first time ever."

- Ask: *What does she mean when she says this?* When Rocket uses the word 'seen' she means he sees her *as a person* and understands how she feels. He can 'see' how much the meteor shower meant to her and how upset she is.

- Next, ask: *How does the illustrator show what Jamal and Rocket are feeling on this page?* Their faces are highlighted in the torchlight and the surrounding page is dark to accentuate the contrast. Jamal is wide-eyed with concern as he looks at Rocket. For once *she* is looking down, showing how sad she is.

- Ask the children to write two sentences: one as Jamal and one as Rocket, explaining how they're feeling at this point. Invite children to share their sentences.

- Ask why it is amazing that Jamal has turned his phone off. (Until now, Jamal has been 'glued' to his phone.)

- Rocket apologises to Jamal for making him wait for nothing. Ask *Why do you think Rocket's apology is also important?* Answers could include that she feels guilty for making him take her out, and it's the first time Rocket has thought of Jamal's feelings and perhaps this wasn't how he wanted to spend his evening but he did it for her.

- Now ask the children to write another two sentences: showing how the characters are feeling now. Share the children's sentences.

- Finally, ask the children what the change in their feelings and actions tells us about their relationship – in the past and how it might be in the future.

5. My hero

Objective
To participate in discussion about what is read to them, taking turns and listening to what others say.

What you need
Copies of *Look Up!*, photocopiable page 21 'My hero'.

Cross-curricular links
PSHE, art and design

What to do

- Look at the third spread with the class, particularly the right-hand page. In this, we see that Rocket admires the astronaut Mae Jemison and wants to be like her when she grows up.

- Explain to the children that when we really admire someone, they become a hero or role model to us, and we can call this 'looking up' to them. Therefore, the title of the book has another interesting meaning.

- Ask the children why they think Rocket looks up to Mae Jemison so much. Answers could include that she was the first African-American astronaut in space, that she's female, and that she overcame a big fear to achieve her aim.

- Next, hand out photocopiable page 21 'My hero'. Tell the children you want them to think about who they admire most, and why. Some children might think of people they know from the internet or television, but they needn't be someone famous. A hero can be a family member, a friend or someone in the community they know.

- On the page, they should write a few sentences about who their hero is and why. What makes them special? How are they inspirational? They can write down any facts here, too, using the internet to research their hero if they are someone famous. If they choose someone they know, they can use their own knowledge instead. There is space on the sheet to draw a picture of their chosen person, too.

Differentiation
Support: Children could just write the name of their hero and a sentence or two.

6. Up or down?

Objective
To articulate and justify answers, arguments and opinions.

What you need
Copies of *Look Up!*

Cross-curricular links
PSHE

What to do

- Look at spread 5 with the children, which shows Rocket and Jamal walking down the street on their way to the supermarket. Tell them just to focus on the illustrations, not the words.

- Ask: *What do you notice about the people on the street? What are the adults and the children doing?* (All the adults seem to be preoccupied with doing something else while they are walking. Most are on phones – either talking on them or looking down at them, although there is one man who has his head in a newspaper. There is one other child apart from Rocket and both are looking around them and noticing their surroundings.)

- Ask the children why the author and illustrator might have chosen to represent the people in this way in this picture. Are they trying to tell the reader something? Answers could include that adults tend to be too busy to notice their surroundings, or that they don't bother to look around, whereas children are interested in what is going on around them. The adults might miss out on interesting or exciting things because they're just not paying attention.

- Next, ask the children if this is what they see when they go out with their friends and families. Are people – especially adults and teenagers – always on their phones? If so, what opinions do the children have about this? Is it good or bad to be on your phone all the time? What are the pros and cons of this? Give children time, in pairs, to come up with either at least two pros or two cons.

- If your class feels confident, you could host a debate with children arguing for or against people using their phones too much in public.

 **Space menu**

In space, astronauts eat three main meals a day like we do on Earth. But, as there is no gravity, they have to eat their food differently.

Some foods can be eaten fresh, like fruit, but main meals come ready-made in packets that astronauts add water to.

Astronauts can choose from lots of different foods, including their favourites. British astronaut Tim Peake asked a famous chef to make him a special bacon sandwich that he could take to space!

However, bread isn't good in space because crumbs can get into the equipment. Instead, flatbreads are used. That is how astronaut Terry Virts created his very own 'space cheeseburger' – by putting beef, cheese, tomato paste and mustard into a wrap!

A space cheeseburger

Most drinks are allowed on board. If an astronaut wants milk or sugar in their tea or coffee, it has to be added before blast-off: you cannot stir milk and sugar into a cup of tea in space!

> ● What would you want to eat in space? On a piece of paper, write down your choices for breakfast, lunch and dinner – together with your favourite snacks and drinks.

My hero

● Who inspires you in life? Draw a picture of your hero and complete the sentences below.

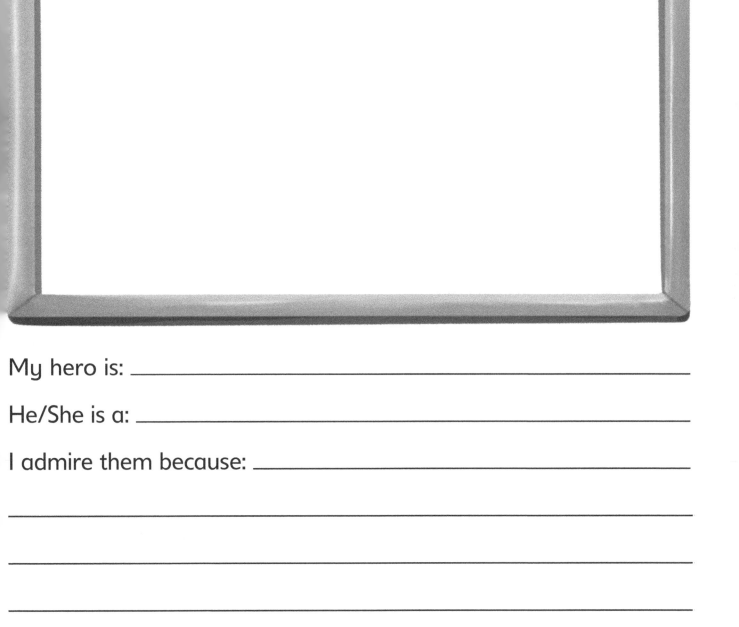

My hero is: _____

He/She is a: _____

I admire them because: _____

_____

_____

_____

_____

TALK ABOUT IT ▶

1. Do a little dance

Objective
To be encouraged to link what they read or hear to their own experiences.

What you need
Copies of *Look Up!*

Cross-curricular links
PSHE, PE

What to do

- To start, look at the right-hand page of spread 9, where Rocket does her 'famous victory dance'. Ask the children why Rocket does this. (It's a way of celebrating getting her own way.) Why does Rocket describe it as 'famous'? (This is a hint that she has done this dance before.)

- Next, ask: *What kind of moves would you use in a victory dance?* In pairs, ask children to discuss this; they can look at the illustrations to help them with their answers. Discuss their ideas as a class. Generally, the moves will be happy ones, with positive body language: arms raised, possibly fast moving and lively. Ask the class to stand up and dance as if they are very happy about something. You can put on some happy music to make this more interactive and fun.

- Then, ask the children what the opposite – a defeat dance – would look like. Again, ask them to discuss in pairs before coming back to share ideas as a class. Suggestions could include slower movements, droopy limbs, a sad expression, hardly moving. Ask the children to now dance as if they are disappointed about something. Again, you could put on some music – slower or sad – to help get them into the mood.

- Finally, ask the children if they ever dance at home to show how they're feeling. Brave volunteers could show the rest of the class how they might celebrate a victory.

2. Expressing yourself

Objective
To gain, maintain and monitor the interest of the listener(s).

What you need
Copies of *Look Up!,* individual whiteboards and pens.

Cross-curricular link
Drama

What to do

- Explain to the children that an essential part of reading aloud is to get the listeners' attention. You do this through not only saying the words correctly but also by adding interest to them through how you say them. For example, if you read in a loud voice, you might want the listener to be frightened or surprised. A silly voice might make the reading funnier.

- Tell the children that you are going to read aloud a passage from *Look Up!* and you want them to give you an honest score out of 5 for how well you read it (5 being the highest). Ask them to write the score on their whiteboard.

- Read any extract where Rocket is excited about seeing the meteor shower. The first time you read it, use a lot of expression and intonation – don't be frightened of exaggerating! Then, ask the children to show their scores for your performance (they should score you 4 or 5).

- Next, read out the same passage in the most boring voice possible – try a monotone. Ask the children to score you on this (you should score no more than 1 or 2). Then, ask the children which performance they liked best and why.

- In small groups, ask children to take turns to read extracts from the book. Finally, invite children to read their extracts to the class, praising them for appropriate expression and intonation.

3. Sibling rivalry!

Objective

To participate in discussions, presentations, performances, role play, improvisations and debates.

What you need

Copies of *Look Up!*

Cross-curricular link

PSHE

What to do

- Tell children that you are going to re-read *Look Up!* to them and, this time, you want them to think about how Rocket and Jamal's relationship is portrayed, through both pictures and words.
- After you have finished reading the book, write the following questions on the board:
  - *Do Rocket and Jamal like each other at the beginning of the book?*
  - *How does Jamal feels about his sister?*
  - *Is Jamal cross when Rocket takes the microphone in the supermarket?*
  - *Why is Jamal annoyed when he gets splashed by water?*
  - *What kind of sister is Rocket to Jamal?*
  - *How does their relationship change at the end of the book?*
- Ask the children for their opinions on these questions and the brother/sister relationship. (Rocket and Jamal probably have a typical sibling relationship – they annoy or ignore each other! Jamal might be fed up with his sister's constant talking about space and then angry when she makes fun of him. Rocket probably feels her brother isn't interested in her, which can make her sad. By the end, they both are more aware of each other's feelings.)
- Next, split the children into pairs. One should be Rocket and the other Jamal. They should think about how each character feels and how they would ask and answer the questions.
- Call the class back together again. Ask for some volunteers to perform the role play.

Differentiation

Support: Children could just describe what kind of character Rocket and/or Jamal is.

4. Press conference

Objective

To consider and evaluate different viewpoints, attending to and building on the contributions of others.

What you need

Copies of *Look Up!*, individual whiteboards and pens, internet access.

What to do

- Look at the right-hand page of spread 4. Point out the sign on the cardboard box that says 'Press Meeting', the microphone, and the toys lined up to listen, with the labels 'Press' on them.
- Ask the children if they know what a Press Meeting or Press Conference is, or if they can guess from the illustrations. Then, explain that it is an event where people from the 'press' (news providers such as TV programmes, websites, newspapers and radio) come along to events to hear someone talk and give information or make an announcement. The press usually asks questions at the end. You could show an example of a press conference on the internet to give them an idea.
- Ask the children: *What is Rocket's Press Meeting about?* (the Phoenix Meteor Shower)
- Next, brainstorm the kind of questions the press might ask Rocket: *These could include: What is a meteor shower? What time will it happen? Why is this exciting and important? Where is the best place to see the shower? How do you know so much about meteor showers?* (This information can be found in the book.) The children can write these down on their whiteboards.
- Tell the children you want them to pretend to be Rocket and to plan a brief speech for a press meeting. They can write what they want to talk about on their whiteboards and use the questions for the press as examples of information to prepare. At the end of the lesson, ask for a few volunteers to be Rocket and for the rest of the class to be the press.

5. My name is...

Objective
To give well-structured descriptions, explanations and narratives for different purposes, including for expressing feelings.
What you need
Copies of *Look Up!*, individual whiteboards, photocopiable page 25 'My name is…'

What to do

- Start the lesson by talking about Rocket's name. Do the children like it? Why or why not?

- Tell children that sometimes people are given a name for a special reason. For example, Rocket is named after a rocket that blasted into space the day she was born. Explain that others may have been named after someone in their family or someone inspirational or famous, or their name may have a special meaning. Often, parents just like a particular name and that's why they choose it. Do the children know why their parents chose their names?

- Next, look at the names that popular superheroes have that show their strength or characteristic, for example: Batman, Wonder Woman, Spiderman. The same is true of comic-book characters such as Traction man, Supertato and Captain Underpants. Can the children give any other examples?

- Hand out photocopiable page 25 'My name is…'. Tell the children that you would like them to come up with a name for a character in a story, and that the name should say something about the character's interests or personality. They can invent a name using imagined powers or description, or they could research names on the internet.

- The children should write the name of their character on the photocopiable page, draw a picture of them, and then write a few sentences about how their character got their name. What does the character's name tell us about them?

- Ask children to present their character to the class, explaining who they are and how they got their name.

Differentiation

Extension: Children could write a short story about their character.

6. Interviewing a star

Objective
To ask relevant questions to extend their understanding and knowledge.
What you need
Copies of *Look Up!*, internet access to written or recorded interviews with Mae Jemison.
Cross-curricular links
PSHE, science

What to do

- Start the lesson by asking the children if they know what an interview is. You might need to explain that it is when one person talks to another about something interesting, such as their life, their job or their interests, etc. Sometimes more than one person asks the questions – and more than one person may be answering them!

- Tell the children that they are going to think of some questions that they would like to ask Dr Mae Jemison – the first African-American woman to travel into space, and who is also Rocket's idol in the book. You could play some interviews from the internet beforehand, so the children get an idea of what happens in an interview and the sort of questions that others have asked Mae Jemison before.

- Give the children five minutes or so to talk in pairs or small groups about the kinds of questions they might like to ask.

- Call the class back together and ask for examples of questions. Write them on the board. Questions might include: *Why did you want to be an astronaut? What did you have to do in order to become an astronaut? What was it like in space? Did you like it? Would you like to go back again?* Children could also use the knowledge gained from Extract 3 to form questions.

- To make this more fun, you could ask for volunteers to pretend to be Mae Jemison and the class could ask them questions, in a pretend interview.

My name is...

● Imagine you are creating a character for a book. What name would you give them and why? Introduce your character below and draw a picture of what they look like.

My character is called: _____

They are called this because:

_____

_____

_____

_____

GET WRITING ▶

1. Memory game

> **Objective**
> To explain clearly their understanding of what is read to them.
>
> **What you need**
> Copies of *Look Up!*, whiteboards.

What to do

- Tell the children that you are going to give them a fun quiz to see how much they can remember about what happens in *Look Up!*

- Before you start the quiz, either read the book with the children again, or let them look at a copy.

- Divide the children into pairs or small groups and give them whiteboards to write their answers on. Read out and/or write on the board the following questions:
  1. From where does Rocket look at the stars every night?
  2. What was Rocket named after?
  3. What is the name of the meteor shower Rocket wants to see?
  4. Where does Rocket give out her flyers?
  5. What splashes Jamal on the way back home?
  6. What drink do Rocket and Jamal have in the park?

- Read the questions a couple of times to give the children a chance to understand what they mean and think of their answers.

- Once they are finished, go through the answers with the whole class, asking children to suggest answers. Tell the children not to worry if they misspell something.
  (Answers: 1. from her bedroom; 2. from a rocket that blasted into space when she was born; 3. Phoenix; 4. at the supermarket; 5. a car; 6. hot chocolate)

> **Differentiation**
> **Extension:** Invite children to write their own quizzes to test the rest of the class with.

2. Beginnings and endings

> **Objective**
> To begin to punctuate sentences using a capital letter and a full stop, question mark or exclamation mark.
>
> **What you need**
> Individual whiteboards.

What to do

- Start off by asking how a new sentence must always begin (with a capital letter).

- Next, ask the children for the three different punctuation marks that they can use to end a sentence. Write a full stop, an exclamation mark and a question mark on the board. Can they tell you when each would be used? Establish:
  - For normal sentences, you use a full stop.
  - When you are asking a question, you use a question mark. Remind the children that questions often begin with words such as: who, what, when, where, why, how and do.
  - An exclamation mark is used at the end of sentences that show strong emotion, such as surprise, excitement, happiness, anger and fear.

- Next, write the following sentences on the interactive whiteboard:
  - *rocket wants to be an astronaut when she's older*
  - *there's going to be a meteor shower tonight*
  - *where shall we see it*
  - *watch out for the car Jamal*
  - *who is mae jemison*
  - *it's best to see meteors at night*

- Tell the children to write these sentences down, remembering to with capital letters and end with the correct punctuation.

- Go through the answers together.

> **Differentiation**
> **Extension:** Children write their own sentences about *Look Up!* using the correct punctuation and capital letters.

3. Mighty meteors!

Objective

To discuss what they have written with the teacher or other pupils.

What you need

Copies of *Look Up!*, internet access, photocopiable page 29 'Mighty meteors!', individual whiteboards.

Cross-curricular links

Science

What to do

- Ask the children what they can remember about meteor showers from reading the book and then revisit spreads 5 and 6 for reminders in the 'DID YOU KNOW?' bubbles. Examples include:
  - 'Meteor showers happen when the Earth moves through the trail of dust left by a comet.'
  - 'Most meteors are smaller than a grain of sand.'
  - 'Meteors are bits of dust burning up in the atmosphere.'
- Next, show the children some information about meteors and/or meteor showers online. NASA has useful videos and web pages written especially for children. After viewing these, ask the children what they have learned and write down anything they find interesting on the board.

- Then, hand out the photocopiable page 29 'Mighty meteors!' and tell the children that you would like them to write some amazing facts about meteor showers in their own words, using the information in *Look Up!* and anything they have learned from the videos they have watched. Ask the children to number each new point separately so they create a list.

- The children could also use tablets or laptops to look for their own material, if time and resources allow. They could do this activity in pairs or individually.

- Ask volunteers to read out their fascinating facts!

Differentiation

Support: Children can copy three of the facts given in *Look Up!*

4. Grand designs

Objective

To write sentences by composing a sentence orally before writing it.

What you need

Copies of *Look Up!*, pictures of rockets from the internet, tablets or laptops, lined paper.

Cross-curricular links

Science, art and design

What to do

- Hand out pieces of lined paper – preferably ones with a blank space at the top or bottom. If this isn't possible, then also hand out blank paper. Tell the children that you would like them to design their very own rocket to take them into space!

- Display some photos or drawings of rockets on the whiteboard or sketch out a quick design of your own. Tell the children this is just to give them an idea of the basic shape and components of a rocket's design.

- Next, explain that the children might like to sketch their rocket first to get an idea of how it would look and any special features it may have, such as things to make it fly faster or higher, or comfortable living spaces. Encourage the children to use their imagination here: the rocket doesn't have to be correct from an engineering point of view! Encourage the children to use the internet or books, if possible, to inspire them.

- Once the children have sketched out their rocket and are happy about its design, tell them to write a few short sentences about their rocket. Things they could include are:
  - how many astronauts it will carry
  - how far it will go
  - the main features – for example, engines, windows, wings, etc.
  - anything that makes it interesting or different
  - a name!
- They should plan what they want to say before committing their ideas properly to paper.

Differentiation

Support: Children could label their rockets instead of writing sentences.

5. Read all about it!

Objective
To sequence sentences to form short narratives.

What you need
Copies of *Look Up!*, photocopiable page 30 'Read all about it!', internet access, old newspapers.

What to do

- Ask the children what the three main parts of a story are (a beginning, a middle and an end). To consolidate understanding, ask what happens at the beginning, the middle and the end in *Look Up!* (Rocket plans to see the Phoenix Meteor Shower; she hands out flyers to people at the supermarket; she goes to the park at night and sees the shower.) Explain that sometimes we refer to this structure as a 'narrative'.

- Next, tell the children that articles in newspapers or on websites often follow the same structure. They introduce a piece of news, give more details, and then end by giving any further information or summarising what they have said. Show the children some examples from child-friendly news sources.

- Hand out photocopiable page 30 'Read all about it!' Tell the children that you would like them to write a newspaper article for the day after the meteor shower. They can write about any or all of the following (the information they need will be in the book):
  - what the meteor shower was called
  - why meteor showers happen/what they are
  - why people turned up to watch the meteor shower in the park
  - what the shower looked like (they will have to use their imaginations!)
  - who Rocket is and why she was important. (You might want to write these on the board for reference.)

- Children can draw a picture in the blank space, as though it were a photo, to accompany their story.

- Share children's stories when they are finished. Their work could also make a visually engaging classroom display.

6. In my opinion...

Objective
To consider what they are going to write before beginning by encapsulating what they want to say, sentence by sentence.

What you need
Copies of *Look Up!*, blank book-review template, art materials, examples of book reviews (preferably written by children).

Cross-curricular links
Art and design

What to do

- Tell the children that they are going to write a book review about *Look Up!*

- Before starting, ask if they know what a book review is. Explain that a good book review:
  - summarises what the book is about (without giving away the ending!)
  - says something about the main character(s)
  - tells you what is good/bad about the book
  - gives an honest opinion.

- Show the children some examples by searching for 'children's book reviews' on the internet. (There are sites where children have written reviews of books – it would be worth having these ready before the start of the lesson.)

- Read out the reviews and ask the children why the reviews are helpful, or not. Have the children read any of the books mentioned? Do they agree with the reviews?

- Next, hand out copies of the blank book-review template and ask the children to fill it in, covering the details you have just discussed. They should include the following information:
  - title of the book
  - name of the author and illustrator
  - what the book is about
  - why they liked the book (or not!)
  - whether they recommend the book. They could also illustrate their review.

Differentiation

Support: Children can write a sentence or two about the book and draw a picture.

Extension: Children could write more reviews about other books they have read.

Mighty meteors!

What amazing facts do you know about meteors and meteor showers? Use the space below to share your knowledge.

What I know about meteors and meteor showers:

_____

_____

_____

_____

_____

_____

_____

_____

_____

Read all about it!

● Write a newspaper article about the Phoenix Meteor Shower. You could include Rocket in it.

THE DAILY PLANET

ASSESSMENT ▶

1. Bigger and better

Objective
To learn how to use expanded noun phrases to describe and specify.

What you need
Copies of *Look Up!*, individual whiteboards.

What to do

- Ask the children if they know or can remember what an expanded noun phrase is (a noun with one or more adjectives describing it). Write some examples on the board, starting with something simple and moving to more detailed ones, for example:
  - the sky
  - the huge, dark sky
  - the huge, dark, star-filled sky.

- Ask the children which one they like best. Can they think of different ways to describe the sky? Write their suggestions on the board.

- Next, tell the children that there aren't many expanded noun phrases in *Look Up!*, except for the following: 'the freezing cold', 'a big bright light', 'the amazing Phoenix Meteor Shower'.

- Ask the children to try writing some expanded noun phrases that could be included in the book. They can write about any nouns they like, but you might want to give them some examples to get started; for example: Rocket's telescope, the park, the supermarket, the meteor shower.

- Children can work individually or in pairs for this activity. They should write their ideas down on their whiteboards and then share them with the class.

Differentiation
Support: Provide children with specific examples (see the examples above).

2. Find the missing letters

Objective
To read words with contractions [for example, I'm, I'll, we'll] and understand that the apostrophe represents the omitted letter(s).

What you need
Copies of *Look Up!*, individual whiteboards.

What to do

- Start the lesson with a reminder that a contraction makes two words into one by leaving out one or more letters and adding an apostrophe.

- Write the following sentences on the board: 'Jamal says I'm called Rocket because I've got fiery breath. But Mum says it's because a famous rocket blasted into space the day I was born!' Circle the contractions and talk about the words that have been shortened (I'm = I am; I've = I have; it's = it is).

- Explain that we use contractions all the time when we speak because they're shorter and easier to say. Give some examples, such as: *We've not seen any meteor showers before. It's such a shame! It'd be exciting to see one!* Write your sentences on the board and ask the children to identify which words are contractions.

- Write the contractions from the book onto the board: *can't, he's, isn't, we'd, wouldn't, we're, everyone's, didn't, that's, let's there's.*

- Ask the children to write down what the contractions are in their full form and then talk about them as a class.

- You can include *won't* but you will need to explain that this is an irregular contraction because it doesn't follow the usual rules!

Differentiation
Support: Provide children with the full forms and ask them to match them with the contractions on the board.

3. And

> **Objective**
> To develop their understanding of the concepts set out in English Appendix 2 by joining words and joining clauses using 'and'.
>
> **What you need**
> Copies of *Look Up!*

What to do

- Explain that you are going to look at how to use the joining word 'and' in sentences. Explain that a joining word is also known as a conjunction.

- Next, tell the children that the word 'and' can be used in different ways as a joining word: either to add more information to a simple sentence (for example: 'I like apples *and* pears.'), or to join two different phrases or short sentences together (for example: 'In the summer holidays, I went to Spain *and* I also went camping.')

- Explain that by joining two shorter sentences to make one longer sentence, they can make their writing more interesting.

- Write the following sentences on the board.
  1. *Rocket looks up at the sky.*   *Jamal looks down at _____.*
  2. *Jamal is a teenage boy.*   *Rocket is a _____ ___.*
  3. *The sun shines in the day.*   *The stars shine at _____.*
  4. *The car drove through a puddle.*   *Jamal got ____.*
  5. *Jamal looks for the milk.*   *Rocket looks for _____.*

- Ask the children to complete the sentences on the right and then tell them to join the sentences on the left with the ones on the right using the joining word 'and' to make one complete sentence; for example: 'Rocket looks up at the sky and Jamal looks down at his phone.' They should do this for each pair.

- Check the children's work

> **Differentiation**
>
> **Support:** Provide children with the full sentences on the right.
>
> **Extension:** Children can make up their own sentences about *Look Up!*

4. Strange sayings (colloquialisms)

> **Objective**
> To discuss and clarify the meaning of words, linking new meanings to known vocabulary.
>
> **What you need**
> Copies of *Look Up!*

What to do

- Tell the children that sometimes, when we want to make our written or spoken language more interesting, we exaggerate or use funny sayings that aren't really true, but we understand what they mean. For example, someone who is hungry might say: 'I could eat a horse!' We know that they aren't going to eat one, but it tells us just how hungry they are.

- Ask the children if they can think of any examples of their own.

- In *Look Up!* the writer also uses some interesting expressions. Write the following on the board:
  - 'My head is always floating in the clouds.'
  - 'Jamal is still glued to his game.'
  - 'I yell at the top of my lungs.'
  - 'Even the birds are holding their breath.'
  - 'I'm speechless.'

- Explain that these expressions are from the book, but we're not meant to take them literally – for example, Rocket's head isn't really in the clouds and Jamal isn't actually glued to his game!

- Ask the children to work in pairs to see if they can come up with an explanation about what each expression means. They might need to look at their copies of *Look Up!* to see the sayings in their contexts.

- Then call the class back together and go through each saying, checking that the children have understood their non-literal meaning. Accept any answers that are along these lines:
  - I'm always dreaming.
  - Jamal can't stop looking at his phone.
  - I yell as loudly as possible.
  - Everyone (even the birds) is waiting in excitement.
  - I'm so amazed/surprised.